MECHANICS
HEREDITY
HEAT & ENERGY
The BODY
WEATHER
THE MIND
CLOSED
ATOMS
&
MOLECULES
ARCHAEOLOGY

Arnold Roth's CRAZY BOOK OF SCIENCE

ARNOLD ROTH'S CRAZY BOOK OF SCIENCE

Conceived, Designed & Perpetrated by
ARNOLD ROTH

A W. W. NORTON BOOK
Published by GROSSET & DUNLAP, INC.
New York

for Sweet Carrie

Library of Congress Catalog Card Number 72-130848
ISBN 0-448-21403-2 (trade ed.)
ISBN 0-448-26173-1 (library ed.)

Published simultaneously in Canada
Printed in the United States of America

Table of Contents

For some reason, early man thought that he'd better learn how to count.

He used his fingers and toes . . .

. . . until shoes were invented . . .
. . . which left just fingers . . .

or he made notches in a stick . . .
unless he was clumsy,

in which case . . .
. . . he counted his bandages.

When records had to be kept, numbers had to be written.

The Egyptians used a system of pictures, figures, and strokes.

The Babylonians used a simple, but confusing, check mark system.

Which is why there aren't too many Babylonians around today.

The Romans used Roman numerals.

The people of India invented figures which were faster and easier to use than Roman numerals.

1 2 3 4 5 6 7 8 9 10

Then the Arabs invented the numbers we use today—called "Arabic numerals." As with fingers and toes, these numbers work in units of ten.

ARABIC NUMERALS

1	2	3	4	5	6	7	8	9	10

Using numbers we can do arithmetic—or mathematical calculations—such as:

The ancient Greeks did great work in measuring shapes. It is called GEOMETRY.

A TRIANGLE is a figure of three straight lines, joined at three points, forming three sets of angles. The use and relations of triangles is called TRIGONOMETRY and it is vital in navigation.

But you've got to know what you're doing.

Two Frenchmen, Viete and Descartes, did major work using letters and number symbols. It is called ALGEBRA. Here is a simple example of how algebra works:

$$\boxed{a} + \boxed{a} \times \boxed{3} = \boxed{6}$$

$$\boxed{?} + \boxed{?} \times \boxed{3} = \boxed{6}$$

$$\left(\boxed{6} \div \boxed{3} = \boxed{2}\right)$$

$$\boxed{2} \times \boxed{3} = \boxed{6}$$

$$\boxed{1} + \boxed{1} \times \boxed{3} = \boxed{6}$$

$$\boxed{a} = \boxed{1}$$

Pierre de Fermat, Blaise Pascal, and Harry "Crackers" Saltzman did studies on the "theory of probabilities."

FERMAT

PASCAL

"CRACKERS"

A 3 Act Play

Sir Isaac Newton discovers GRAVITY, leading to measurement of pressures, specific gravity, and other headaches.

Sir Isaac also discovered CALCULUS—which is a method for figuring changing conditions (Gottfried Leibniz *also* discovered calculus—which is more than a lot of people—except Sir Isaac—can say).

Today, electronic computers do much of our mathematical calculating . . .

. . . but you've got to know what you're doing.

Chemistry is one of the oldest sciences. Early man was a chemist when he learned how to take metals from ores.

All three of these men are right in their own way. The chemical symbol for iron is Fe; for tin, Sn; and copper, Cu. Otherwise, the fellow in the middle really is a dummy.

An ancient Greek philosopher, named Aristotle, confused things for a long time when he decided there were only four elements—FIRE, WATER, EARTH, and AIR. The idea caught on immediately though you don't hear it too much today.

FUNNY, FUNNY, ARISTOTLE MAKING ONE BIG MISTAKE

Another ancient Greek philosopher, named Leucippus, and his student, Democritus, thought that matter was composed of atoms. Their theory didn't catch on for over 2,000 years. Good thing Leucippus and Democritus didn't depend on their theories to make a living.

Leucippus and Democritus Making Friends Through Science

In the middle ages the only chemists were the ALCHEMISTS. They tried to turn things into gold. As we now know, gold is an element and cannot be made. Although they did make some chemical discoveries, alchemists were more stubborn than they were smart.

* Don't be fooled—this alchemist is *not* discovering gold foil.

Everything in the world is made of MATTER. Matter exists in three forms—solid, gas, and liquid.

These three forms of matter are called COMPOUNDS.
Compounds are made of MOLECULES.
Molecules are made of ATOMS.
So far, 103 different, natural atoms have been discovered.*
These atoms are called ELEMENTS.

* See ATOMS and MOLECULES, page 39—when you get there.

When different elements are combined in various combinations, the form of their compound can change. Sodium (Na) is a shiny metal and Chlorine (Cl) is a smelly gas. When compounded, they become the chemical Sodium Chloride—commonly known as table salt.

Certain combinations of the chemicals Calcium (Ca), Carbon (C), Chlorine (Cl), Hydrogen (H), Iodine (I), Iron (Fe), Magnesium (Mg), Nitrogen (N), Oxygen (O), Phosphorus (P), Potassium (K), Sodium (Na) and Sulfur (S) produce the strangest compounds ever seen, heard, or contacted.

They also have the strangest names—such as Jim, Charlie, Nancy, Shirley, Mr. and Mrs. Pitkin, Adam, the kid next door, etc., etc.. Chemists, and others call these compounds "people."

A NICHE IN CHEMISTRY'S HALL OF FAME
ROBERT BOYLE
(1627~1691)
"FATHER OF CHEMISTRY"
CHEMISTRY BOYLE
(1657~1923)
"SON OF ROBERT"

An Itch In Everybody's Hall of Fame
The Science of Chemistry affects everything in life today. Whether we want it to, or not.
COUGH KOFF
COUGH
KOFF
COUGH
KOFF
COUGH
COUGH
COUGH COUGH
COUGH COUGH
COUGH COUGH
COUGH
COUGH COUGH COUGH
COUGH
COUGH
COUGH

THE MAD CHEMIST

An Elemental Drama

The practice of medicine is a blend of science and art. Medical Science is concerned with preventing and curing illness. Nature is concerned with curing and preventing medical science.

Witch doctors were the first medical men. They thought disease was caused by evil spirits which lived in the patient's body.

Early Orientals made holes for the evil spirits to use for escape.

HIPPOCRATES denied magic and superstition a place in medicine. Doctors still honor him by taking the Hippocratic Oath.

Modern medicine uses two main methods to treat the illnesses and diseases of the body.

Medication

Surgery

Major Advances In Medicine & Whimsy

Dr. EDWARD JENNER of England discovered that vaccination with cowpox serum prevented the patient from developing the dreaded smallpox.

LOUIS PASTEUR of France proved there was a connection between germs and diseases.

Lord JOSEPH LISTER of England and Scotland discovered antiseptic surgery—making surgery a much more reliable medical treatment.

WILHELM RÖNTGEN of Germany invented the X-ray machine which enables doctors to study people's interiors before doing anything drastic.

WILLIAM DUNAFFEE, Jr. of Boston discovered his mysterious ailments suddenly disappeared when he learned he could go to a Red Sox game.

The discovery of vitamins and studies in nutrition and hygiene teach us how to take care of ourselves and prevent illness.

The boy who didn't eat his right foods.

The boy who ate his right foods.

The boy who ate his right foods—and a lot of others, too!

The dedicated doctor takes care of us no matter when, where, who, or what.

Much medical research is done on animals before a new treatment is used on humans.

Dentistry is rapidly progressing and enlarging.

But the greatest credit for all medical advancement must go to that person without whom all medical endeavor would be wasted .... *the patient.*

CELLS

The first, fairly practical microscope was built by Anton van Leeuwenhoek—which was his second greatest accomplishment. The first was learning to spell his name. Looking through his microscope, he was the first man to see MICROBES—mostly because he was the first man to look through his microscope.

Van Leeuwenhoek looking at a single-cell microbe.

A single-cell microbe looking back at Van Leeuwenhoek.

Newborn babies have over 26,000,000,000,000 cells and fancy names like Agnes and Walter. Cells have fancy names, too—like AMOEBA and PROTOZOA.

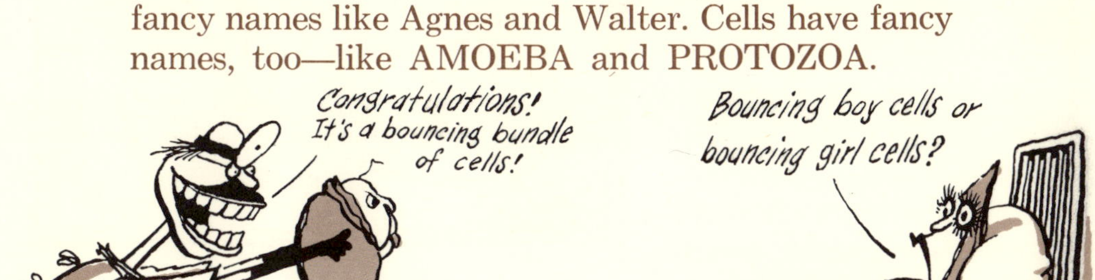

A CELL is the fundamental unit of life. A cell is an energy-charged compound. That is why we must always be nice to cells—even though they make poor pets.

A Peculiar Fellow Talking To Some of His Cells No Matter What People Think

Cells can contain things like protein molecules, amino acids, carbon atoms, ribonucleic acids, etc., but you don't *need* to know that. You do need to *have* cells . . . and the cells will take care of the rest. *They* know who and what they are.

Cells can reproduce themselves by splitting into two identical bodies.

This process is called MITOSIS and is the way that life continues itself.

MITOSIS is occurring constantly in living things.

(Another Stupid frog)

Here is a drawing of an actual cell with the real names of its parts:

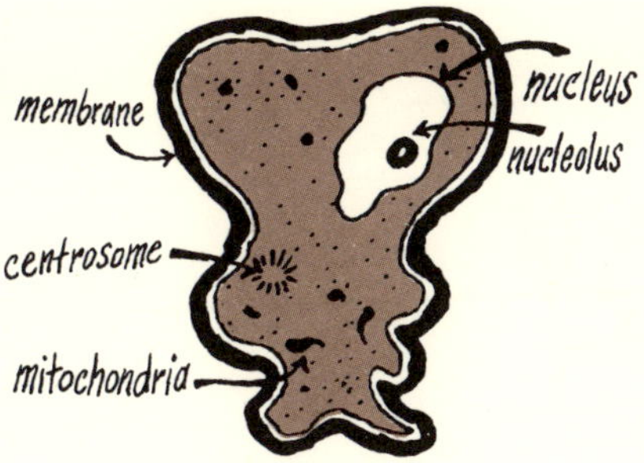

Here is another drawing of an actual cell with the names of its real parts:

All living things are composed of a variety of cells.

Plants have cells.

Animals have cells.

Rocks don't have cells.

HEREDITY is the passing on of physical and psychical characteristics from parents to offspring for better or worse—or, even, worse than that.

An example of heredity at work.

An example of heredity taking things easy.

The founder of the science of heredity (called GENETICS) was an Augustinian monk named Gregor Mendel. He based his work on the study of peas.

The factors which determine hereditary traits are called GENES. There are two kinds of genes:

A dominant gene being bored to tears.

An angry genie

Although genes determine many things about us, other things have influence, also.

The framework of the human body is the SKELETON. The skeleton consists of 206 bones, all of which have funny names which are hard to remember. Here is a sampling of the easier ones.

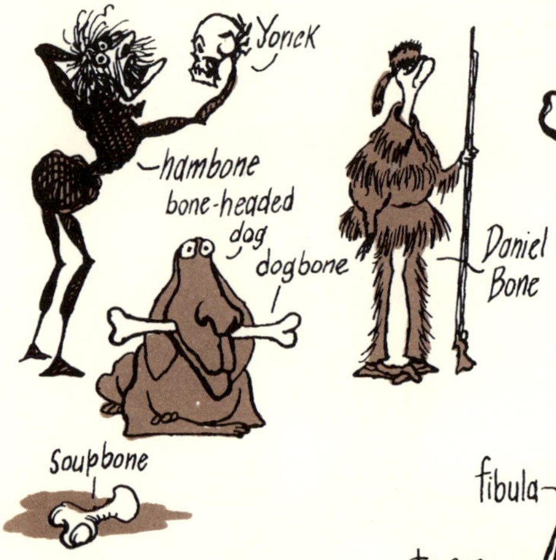

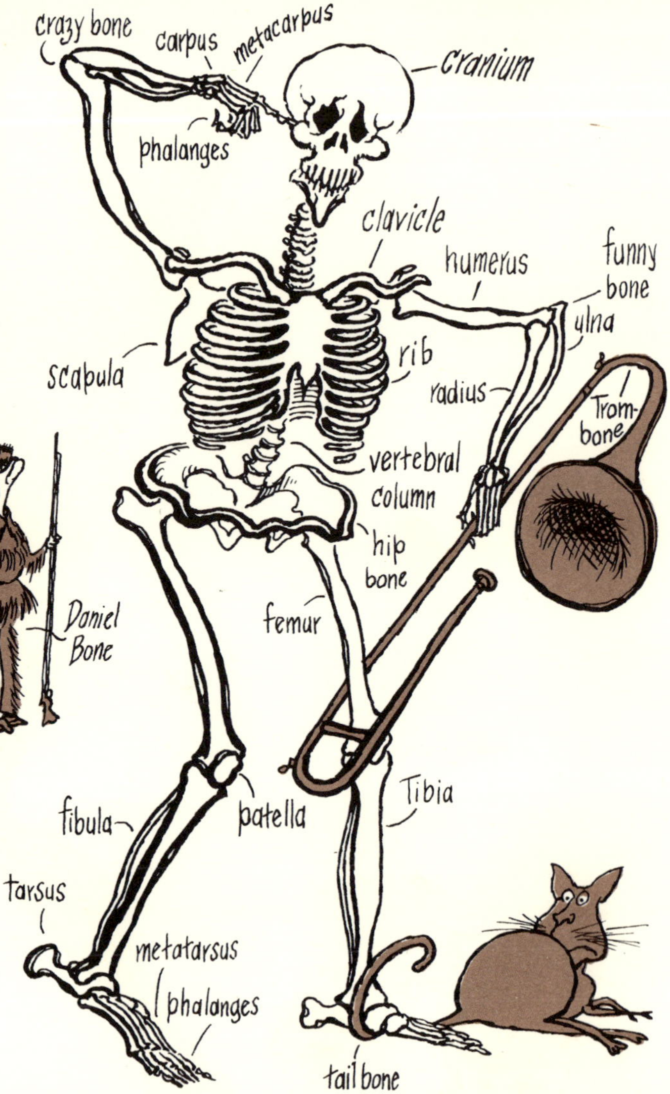

The CIRCULATORY SYSTEM consists of 60,000 miles of tubes (less in kids and midgets) and was designed by a Rumanian road architect. The blood is pumped by the heart through these tubes which are called arteries, arterioles, capillaries, venules, and veins. The blood is returned to the heart which pumps it out again. Hearts are not famous for their imaginations.

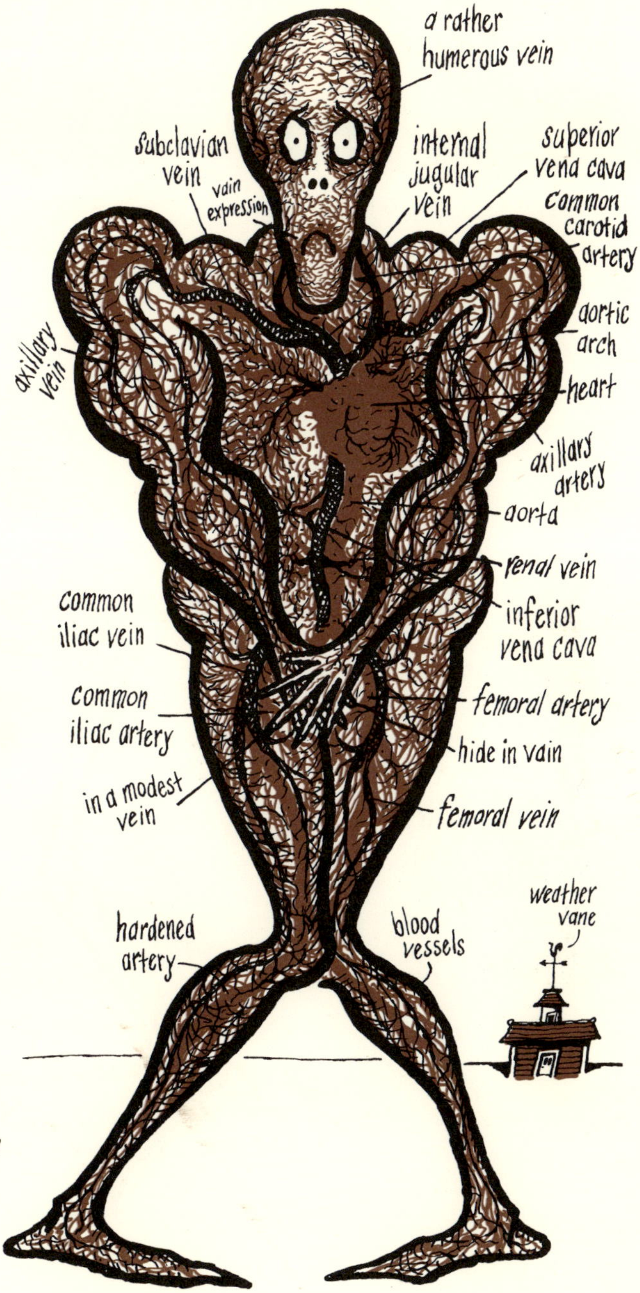

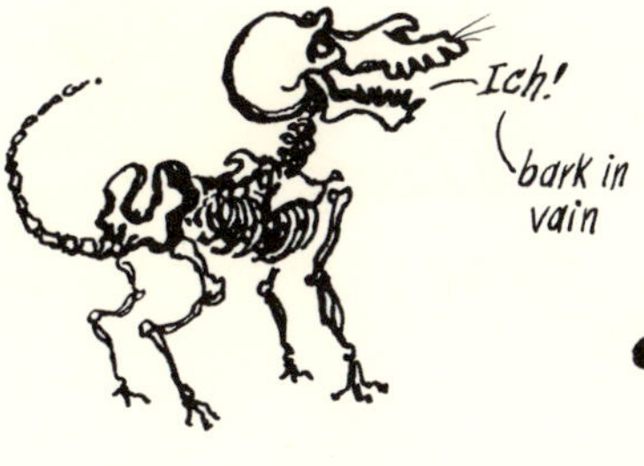

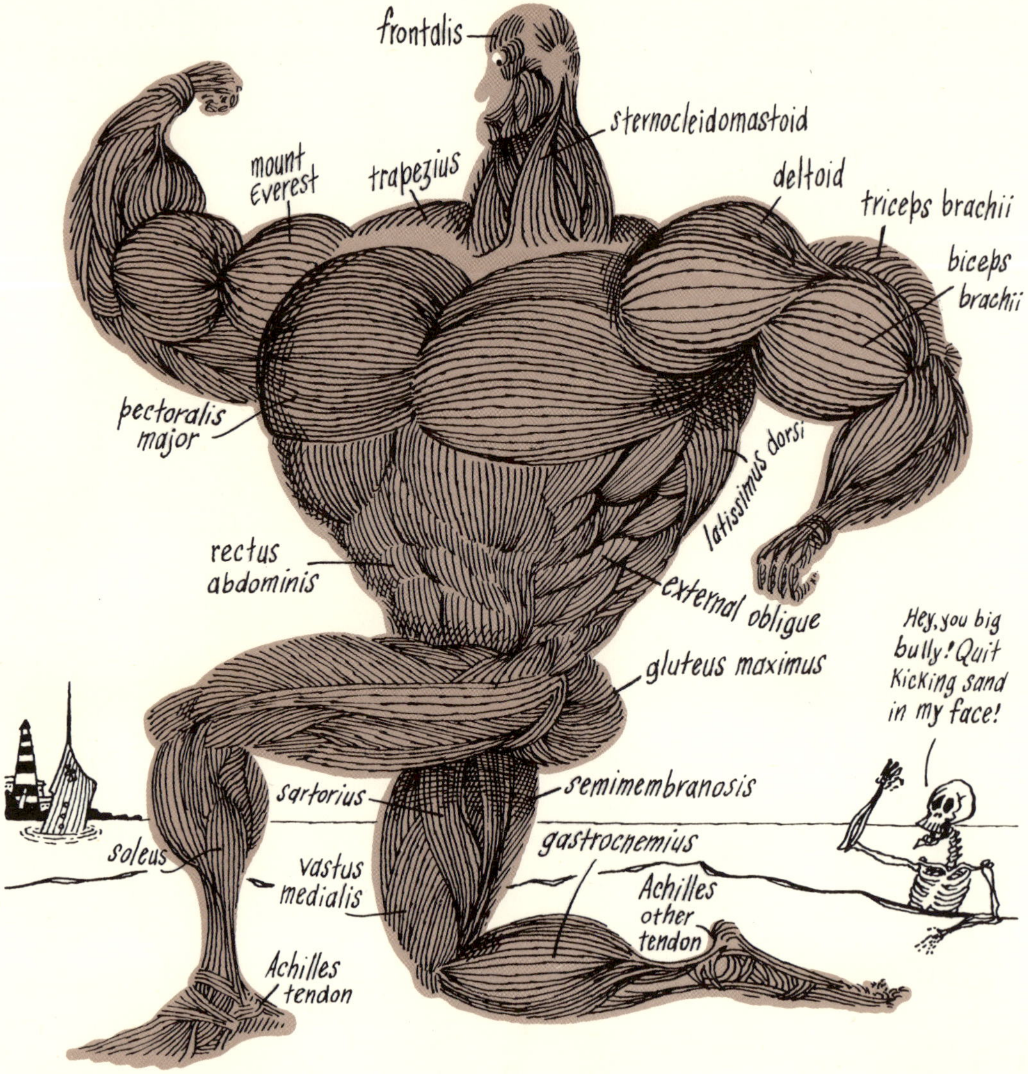

The MUSCLES enable the body to move and, if they are big enough, to bully other people. There are over 600 muscles, all with strange names, hardly any of which are needed to watch television.

The NERVOUS SYSTEM consists of the brain, spinal cord, and nerves. The nerves sense things and send information to the brain. They also carry orders back from the brain to the muscles. They are not to be trusted.

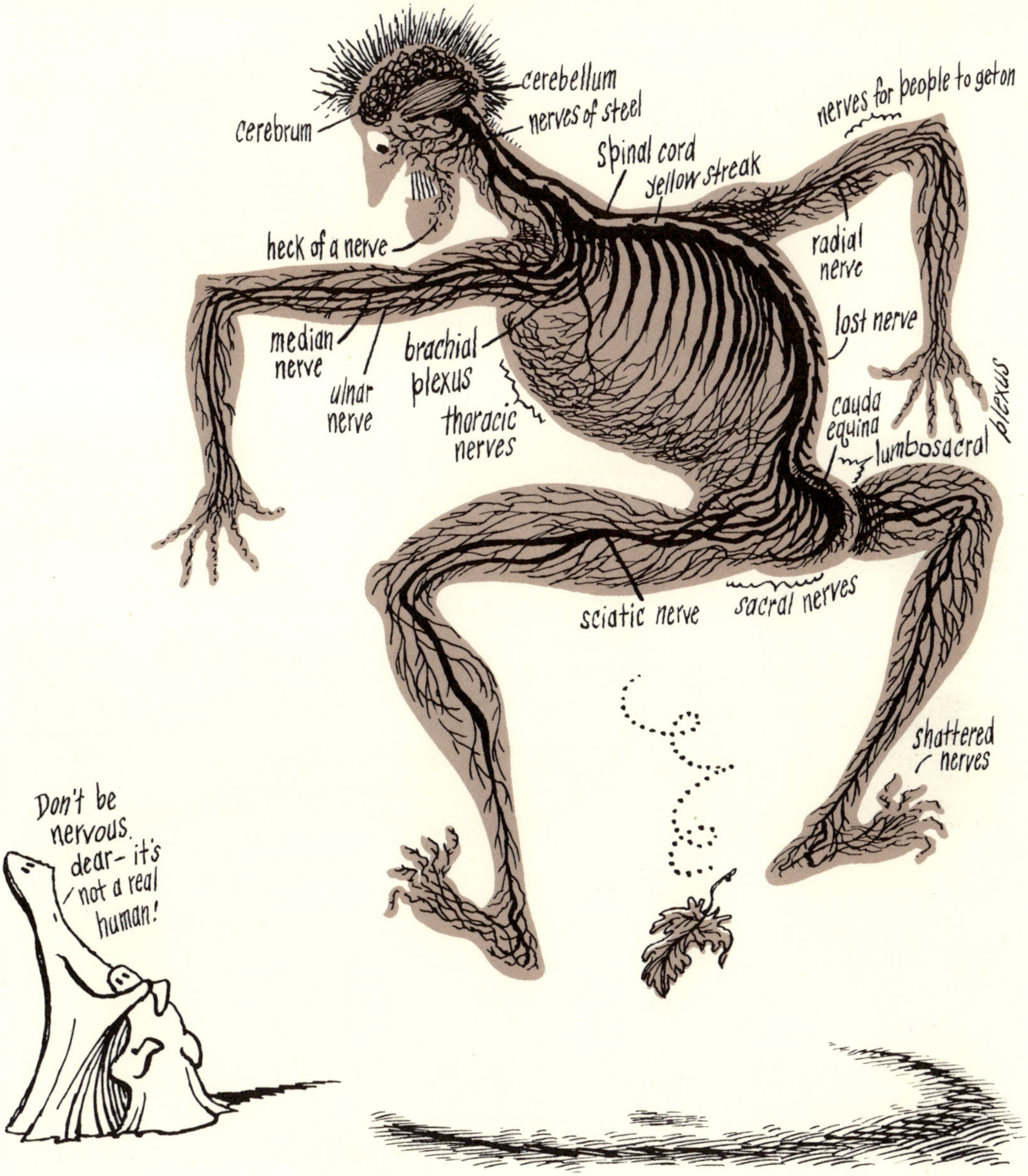

The ORGANS are best remembered because they have the easiest names. Organs are very useful though they are not much to look at. Here are some of the more popular organs in use today:

The basic unit of all matter is the ATOM. Atoms are so small no one has ever seen one. This hasn't stopped people from talking to them, however. If you *could* see one it might look like this:

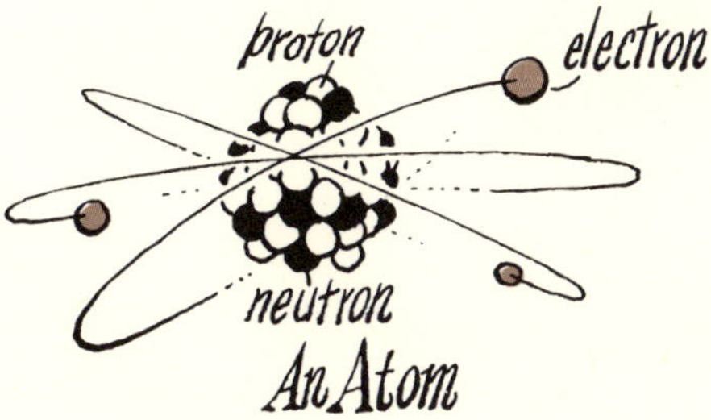

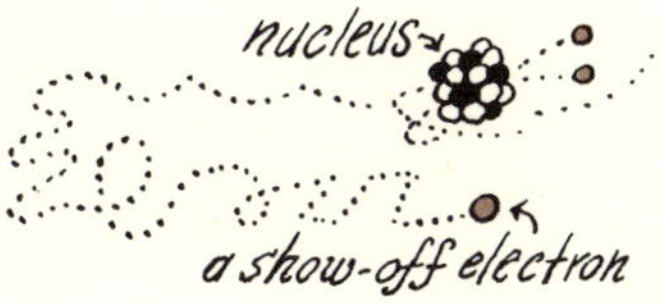

Atoms consist of three parts: protons, neutrons, and electrons. Protons and neutrons cluster together to form the nucleus. The electrons move rapidly around the nucleus.

In 1905, Albert Einstein formulated his Theory of Relativity which, in effect, shows that matter and energy are equivalent. The major part of his formula is $E=MC^2$ (energy equals mass times the speed of light squared). This didn't stop people from talking to Albert Einstein, however.

Atoms are the source of tremendous energy. To get at this power scientists learned to "split" atoms, thereby releasing nuclear energy.

Atom bombs are an example of uncontrolled atom "splitting"—called "chain reaction." Controlled nuclear energy is produced in nuclear reactors. It gives man a new source of power and atoms something new and different to do.

When atoms cluster together they form a MOLECULE.

A Cluster of Atoms

CLUSTER'S LAST STAND

When molecules are heated, they become more active.

HOT MOLECULES EXPERIMENT A

TEST: This lady's molecules have just sat on a hot rock.

PROOF: You can fool some of the molecules all of the time, all of the molecules some of the time, but, don't sit on hot rocks.

When molecules are squeezed into a space, pressure is increased.

SQUEEZED MOLECULES EXPERIMENT A

TEST: This man's molecules are being squeezed.

PROOF: He doesn't like it one bit.

GREAT 20TH CENTURY MOMENTS IN SCIENCELAND

MAN MASTERS THE ATOM

What does the future hold for man and atom?

HEAT & ENERGY

Man always knew there was heat . . .
. . . and there was more heat . . .
. . . and less heat.
He tried various ways . . .
. . . to measure . . .
. . . amounts of heat . . .

. . . but never could do so . . .
. . . with any degree . . .
. . . of constant accuracy.
But, he learned something . . .
. . . from his efforts:
to stop trying.
Except someone like Daniel Gabriel Fahrenheit . . .
. . . who perfected an instrument we've named after him . . .
Here is an honorary degree for you!
32
Could I have a glass of water, instead?
. . . the thermometer.

A HURRIED DEMONSTRATION OF HEAT PROPERTIES USING WATER AS OUR EXAMPLE—AND VICTIM.

Water is a liquid. When the molecular action of water is left pretty much alone, it remains a LIQUID.

A WATER-BASED TRAGEDY

"The Ancient Mariner Looks For Pity"

When the action of the water's molecules is sufficiently slowed—and the water's temperature is decreased enough—the water freezes into ice—a SOLID.

When the temperature of water is increased, tremendous molecular activity is created. The water boils and becomes coffee or tea or an awfully hot bath.

Boiling water does change its form. It turns into steam, which means the molecules are in vapor form—a GAS.

THEORY: Heat is a form of motion.
PROOF:

THEORY: And therefore, a form of energy.
PROOF:

MORAL: You can lead a horse to water, but you can't make him think.

There are various types of sound. Some various types:

LOUD SOUND

SOFT SOUND

HIGH SOUND

LOW SOUND

PUGET SOUND

UNSOUND

It was Robert Boyle (Chemistry's father—remember?) who also proved that sound is carried by the air.

A VERY SOUND ADVENTURE
BOYLE'S PROOF
or
SOUND IS IN THE NOSE OF THE BEE HOLDER

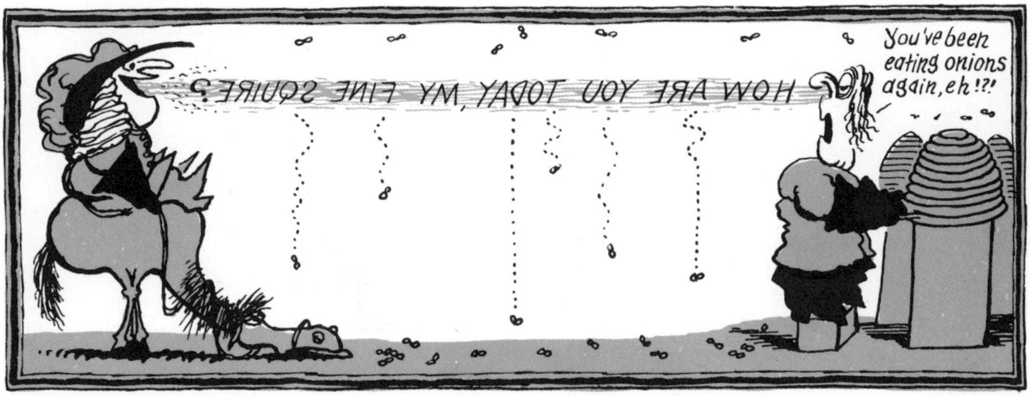

HOW SOUND TRAVELS

Motion (usually of warmer air) compresses layers of air (or water, or gas—though not so well) molecules and the compression ripples through the molecules in waves which scientists call "vibrations" and music lovers call "awful."

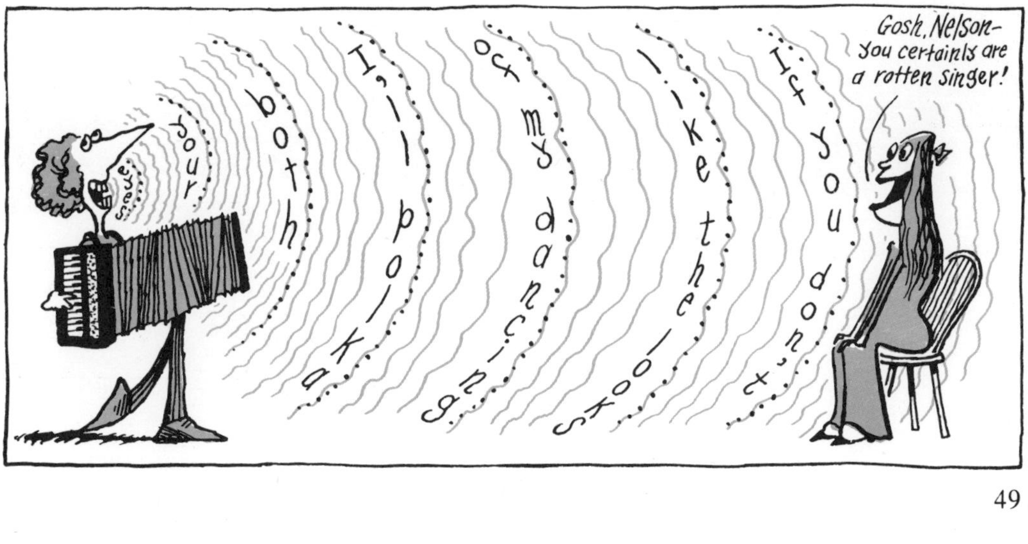

ANOTHER RIPPLE IN VERY SOUND HISTORY

The Speed of Sound Gets Measured or HOW IT WAS PROVED THAT SOUND TRAVELS ABOUT 1100 FEET PER SECOND

Bats, being almost blind, use sound, in a sonar form, as a guide in their flight.

A Flying Bat Using Radar

High-pitched sounds are sent forward by the bat. The rebounding echoes inform the bat of obstacles ahead unless, in addition to being nearly blind, the bat is also deaf.

A Deaf Bat Crashing.

HOW SOUND IS HEARD BY HUMANS, FRIENDS, NEIGHBORS & RELATIVES.

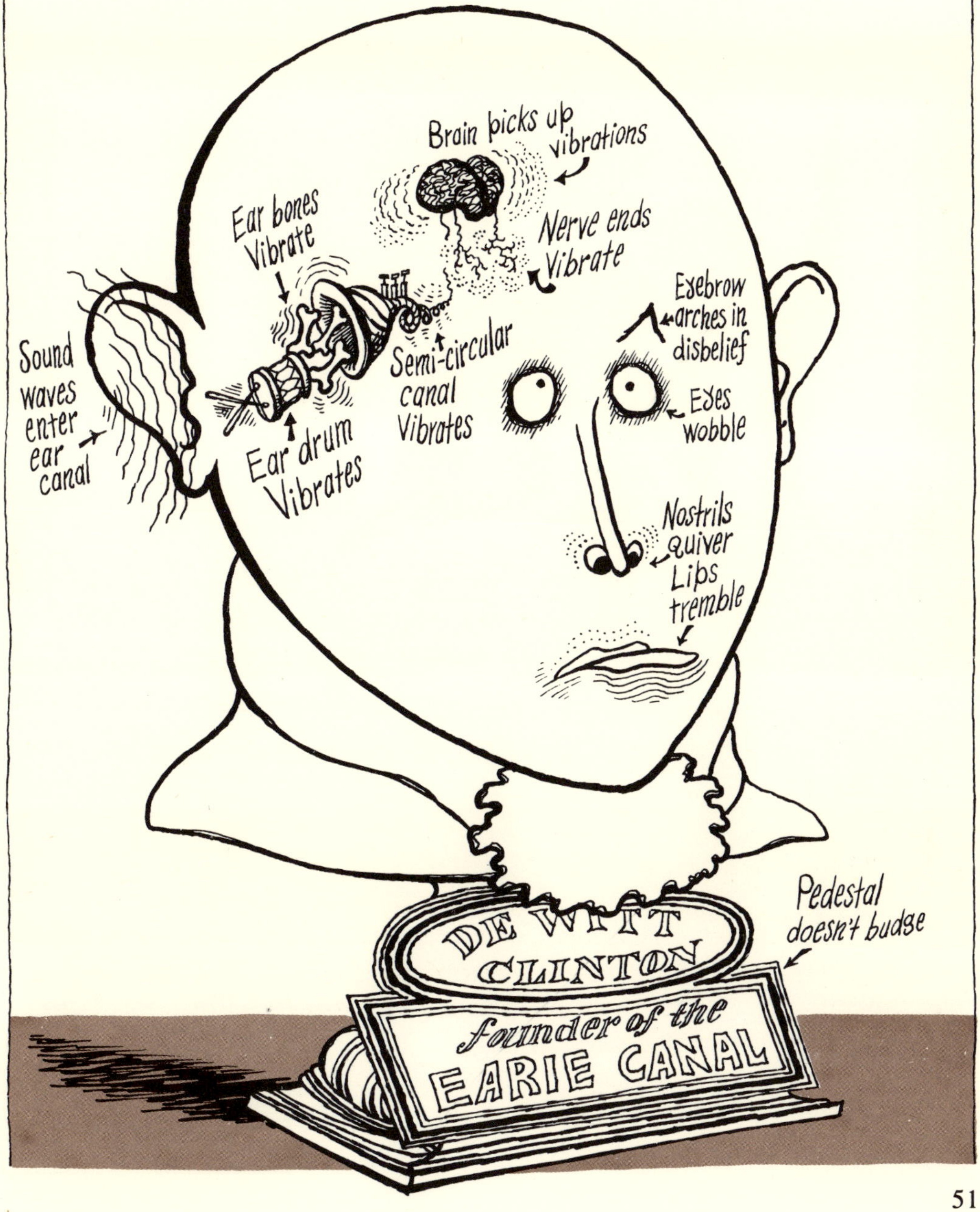

SOUND . . . . . . travels . . . . . . slowly . . .

. . . in . . . . . . cold . . . . . . air.

THE DOPPLER EFFECT PROVED BEYOND DOUBT & HUMAN ENDURANCE that when the source of sound is moving, speed and distance will affect the tonal pitch. Because of variations in the constantly changing distance to the sound source, the tone is higher as it approaches, lower as it recedes.

Think of all the fun we'd miss if there were no sound. Better yet, think of something else.

Because he just can't let things be, man felt he should find a way to measure the progression of natural phenomena. That progression is called TIME.

One of the first clocks was the sundial. But, it wasn't perfect.

The hourglass also had its failings.

The Mayans worked out an ingenious calendar.

The calendar year is based on the time it takes the earth to travel around the sun—which is 365 days, 5 hours, 48 minutes, and 46 seconds. That is why we have leap year every four years and also, why calendar makers grow old before their time.

Galileo found that the swing of a pendulum takes the same amount of time regardless of the length of the swing.

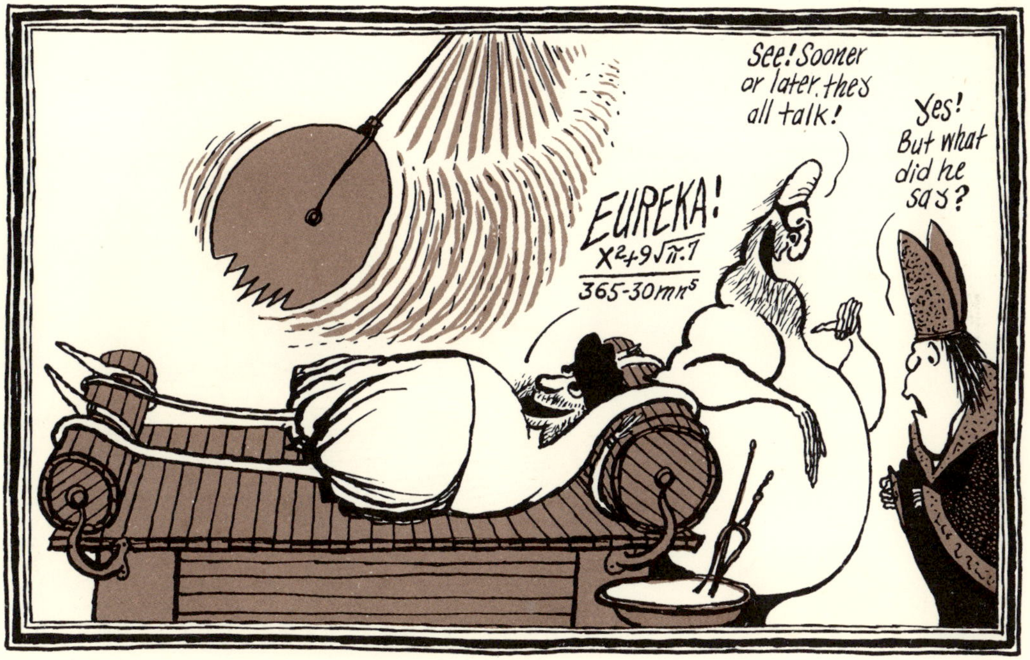

Christiaan Huygens made a great advancement when he designed the balance spring for watches.

HOW A CLOCK WORKS

Tension from the hairspring causes the balance to swing back and forth, like a flat pendulum lying down. This moves the lever which allows the escape wheel to move one section at a time. The mainspring moves the escape wheel which sends an impulse back through the lever to keep the balance wheel moving. The escape wheel moves the gears which control the minute and hour hands. Then, the watch gets dropped and none of this matters.

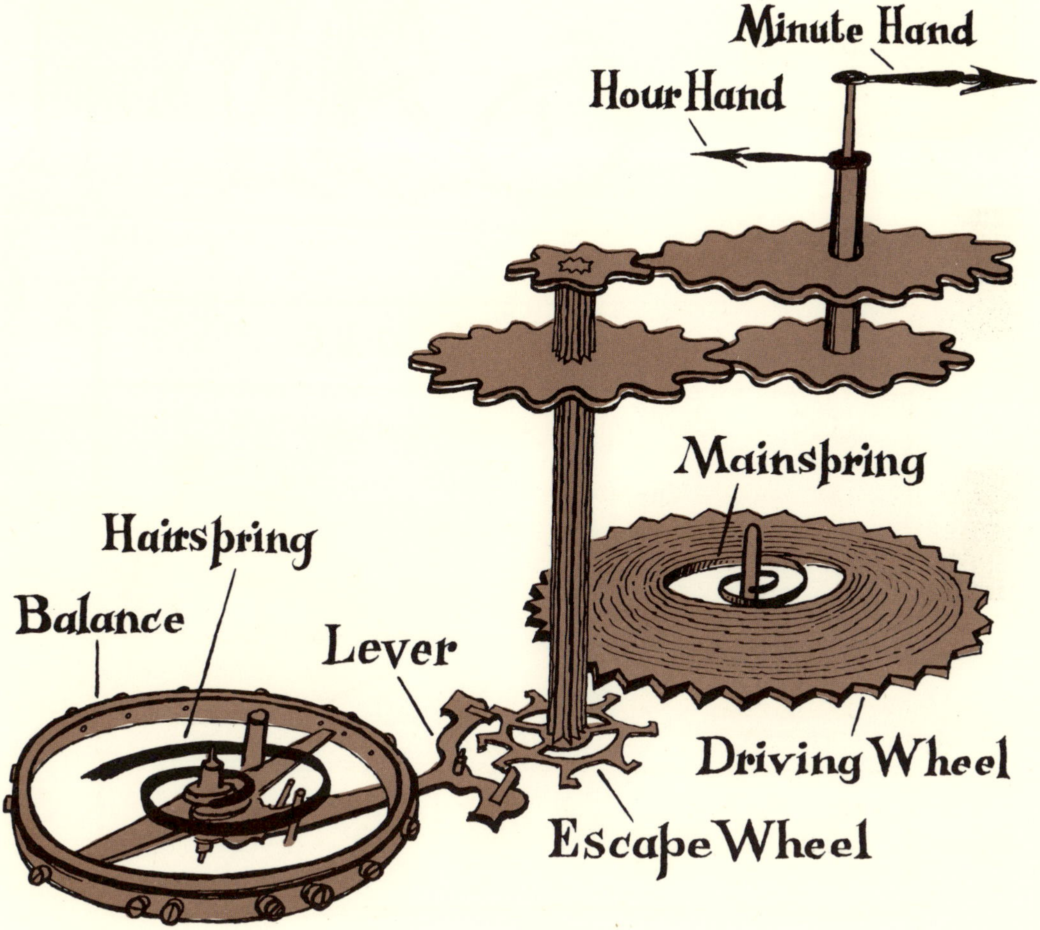

HOW TO FOOL YOUR FRIENDS & MAKE ENEMIES THROUGH TIME

Time provides a good topic for riddles:

What did the wrist watch say to the steeple clock? *Your time is up.*

What has a face and hands and can tell the time? *A watch.*

What did the wrist watch say to the alarm clock? *See you later, aggravator.*

What has a face and hands but can't tell the time? *A broken watch.*

What goes "tick-tock" and falls down a lot? *A drunken Grandfather clock.*

Without light, lenses and prisms would not be very interesting. We know this to be true because, even with light, lenses and prisms are hardly the thrill of a lifetime. It is what light, lenses, and prisms do to each other that interests us.

A Lens & A Prism Having A Light Conversation

Before we can understand much about lenses and prisms and their conversations, we should know something about light.

The air is filled with invisible ELECTROMAGNETIC WAVES (remember SOUND?) (remember MOLECULES?) (remember anything, you dummy?). Some can be heard by the ear. Others through a radio, TV, etc. Others can't be heard at all, luckily.

← A man thinking he can hear an electromagnetic wave.

← A man making electromagnetic waves.

When electromagnetic waves become more frequent they vibrate faster and, eventually, can be felt as HEAT WAVES.

A lady thinking she is listening to a heat wave. →

A lady listening to a heat wave but not hearing anything. →

When the heat waves become more frequent, and the vibrations become faster, they become LIGHT WAVES.

← A man thinking he can hear a light wave.

← A lady still listening for the same heat wave.

Beams of light can be bent in a prism. This phenomenon is called REFRACTION.

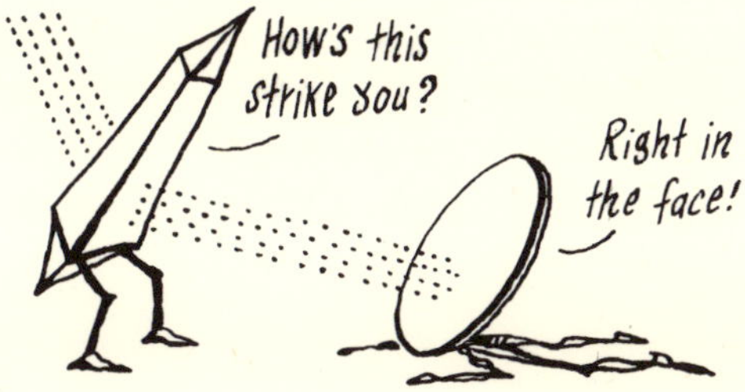

When light rebounds from an object, the result is called REFLECTION. Mirrors reflect—which is more than can be said about a lot of people.

When light strikes a prism in certain ways, the refraction produces a SPECTRUM. A spectrum is a band of colors much like a rainbow. An instrument called the SPECTROSCOPE is used to analyze spectra formed by light reflected from planets and stars. The analysis tells which basic elements are present in those heavenly bodies.

There are two basic types of LENSES.

CONCAVE

A concave lens at rest.

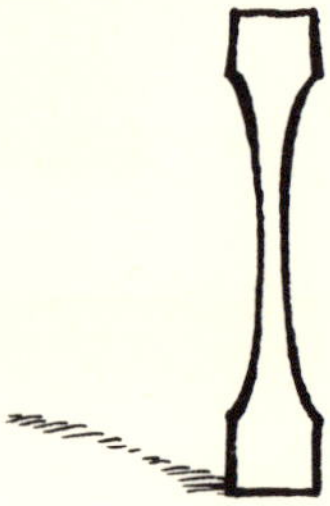

A concave lens curves in.

A concave lens makes things appear smaller.

CONVEX

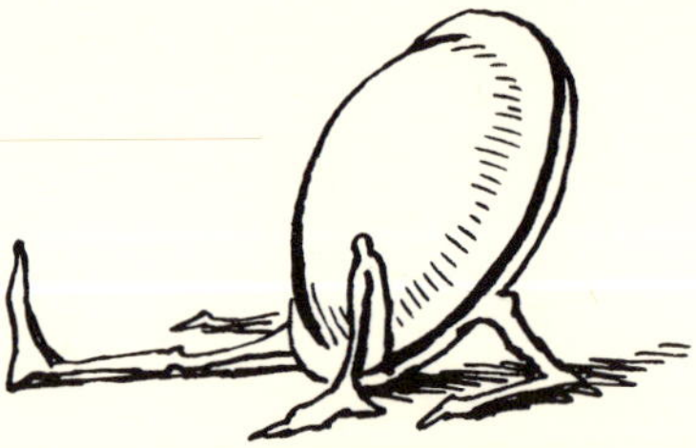

A convex lens not doing much, either.

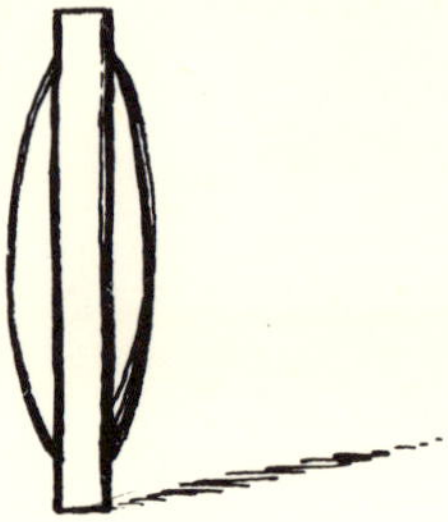

A convex lens curves out.

A convex lens makes things appear larger.

Lenses are used alone or in combination to provide many wonderful instruments for study and fun and, sometimes, both.

ELECTRICITY was discovered by a caveman named Albert C. Drngblv.

He mistakenly called it "ooch."

Albert also discovered caves . . .

. . . and never mentioned ELECTRICITY again.

And, so, for a long time electricity was all but . . .

. . . forgotten.

People noticed that a piece of glass, rubbed on silk, produced sparks. Sometimes bits of wool, paper, etc., were pulled toward the glass. We call this pulling action "MAGNETISM." They called these powers "electricity" which was a name they had left over as it wasn't being used for anything else at the time.

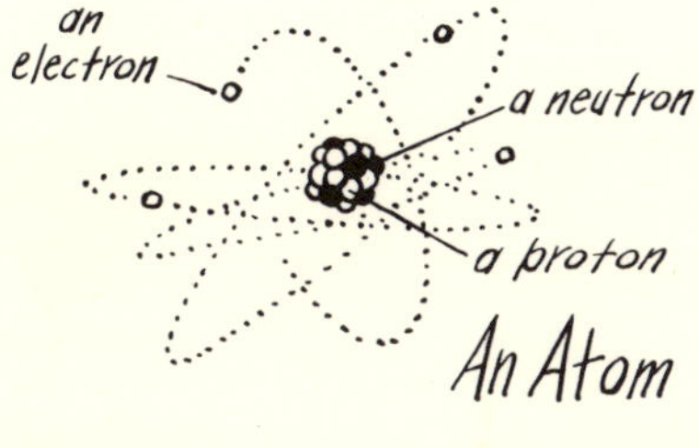

When the number of electrons in an atom are changed, the atom has a magnetic CHARGE. When these charges are channeled we have electric CURRENT.

Anything through which electricity can travel is called an "electric CONDUCTOR." Anything which *won't* conduct electricity is called an "INSULATOR." We also use the word electric to mean "exciting" or "thrilling."

An electric conductor (wire) wrapped in an insulator (rubber).

An electrifying conductor.

An electrified orchestra.

Benjamin Franklin, using a wet string as a conductor, a grip of silk thread for an insulator, and a metal key as a TERMINAL, discovered that lightning is electricity. He told everyone about it which is why we still remember Benjamin Franklin but not Albert C. Drngblv.

Franklin also invented the lightning rod to prevent lightning from setting houses on fire.

Soon, it was found that chemicals would produce electricity—which is what happens in BATTERIES.

A flashlight battery

An automobile battery

A baseball battery

GENERATORS produce electricity by passing magnets near coiled wires. Rabbits, on the other hand, do not produce electricity at all—just more rabbits.

Two electric generators

Two rabbit generations

Using electricity, Alexander Graham Bell invented the telephone.

AN ELECTRIFYING MOMENT IN HISTORY
The First Dull Telephone Conversation (above).

An electrical wizard, Thomas Alva Edison, invented:

and many, many other electric wonders.

Electricity and electric items should *not* be tampered with by anyone who does not understand exactly what he is doing. And that means YOU, too. Remember Albert C. Drngblv—and *he* was lucky.

Today, many things we use are run by electricity.

An Elective Quiz On Electricity

Prove Your Knowledge, Ignorance, or Unconcern About Electricity
What You Don't Know Can't Help You

		true	false
1.	Atoms have protons, neutrons, electrons, and Adam's apples.	☐	☐
2.	An electron is when you vote.	☐	☐
3.	An electron is when you *don't* vote?	☐	☐
4.	Benjamin Franklin invented lightning.	☐	☐
5.	Thomas Alva Edison invented lightning.	☐	☐
6.	Benjamin Franklin invented Thomas Alva Edison.	☐	☐
7.	Electricity is man's best friend.	☐	☐
8.	Electricity doesn't have a best friend.	☐	☐

How to Score: All "true" answers are false. All "false" answers are, naturally, false answers. All other answers are from some other quiz.

MECHANICS

For ages man dreamed of having something else do his work for him.

That something else was MECHANICS. Mechanics deals with the working of engines and machines. Man always understood the basic mechanics of what it was he wanted to do but he lacked sufficient energy to do it.

THE UNENERGETIC MECHANICAL WORLD ("the Old Days")

With hard work and lucky guesses, man learned the secrets of energy and how to use them. He produced engines to operate his machines.

A STEAM ENGINE

AN ELECTRIC ENGINE

AN INTERNAL COMBUSTION ENGINE

A JET ENGINE

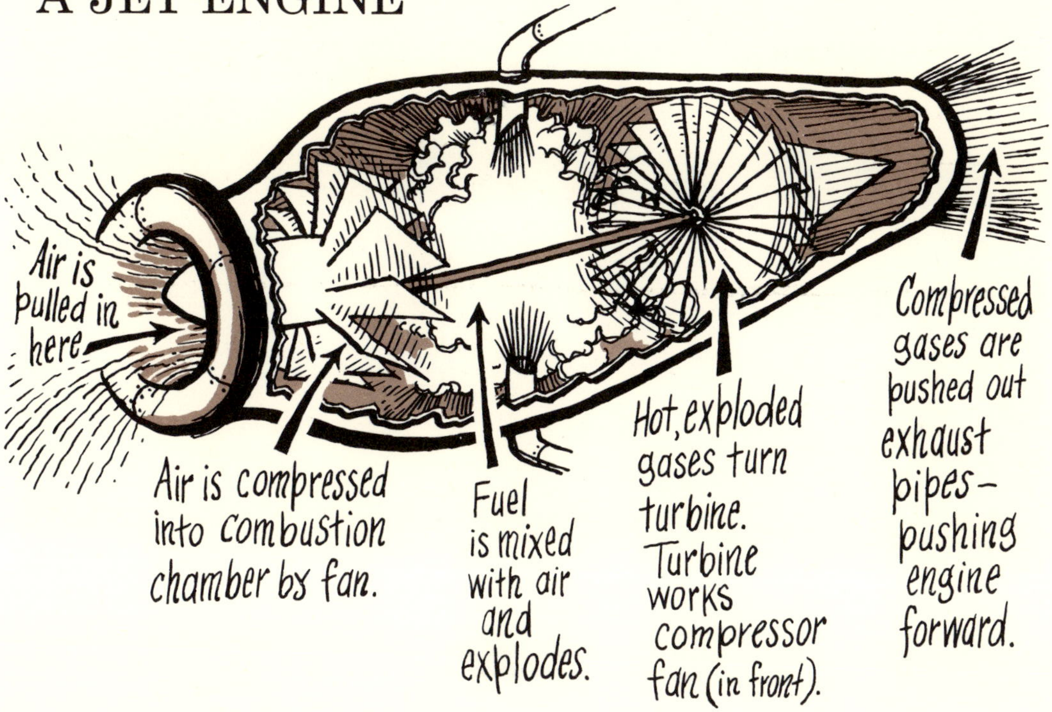

Now that man has engines to do his work for him, he is happy and content.

There are different theories on how our universe originated.

Some think it was the result of a gas explosion.

Others think it was the joining together of gases.

Many don't think about it at all.

People who study the heavenly bodies are called ASTRONOMERS.

Finding out about space has been an uphill battle all the way. An ancient astronomer named Ptolemy tried hard but came up with some wrong guesses and silly conversations.

Galileo told everyone the truth: The Earth travels around the Sun.

A lot of good it did him.

Galileo was more right than he knew. The Earth turns completely around once every day. It takes a year for the Earth to go completely around the Sun.

There are nine planets in our solar system. All but Earth are named after Greek Gods.

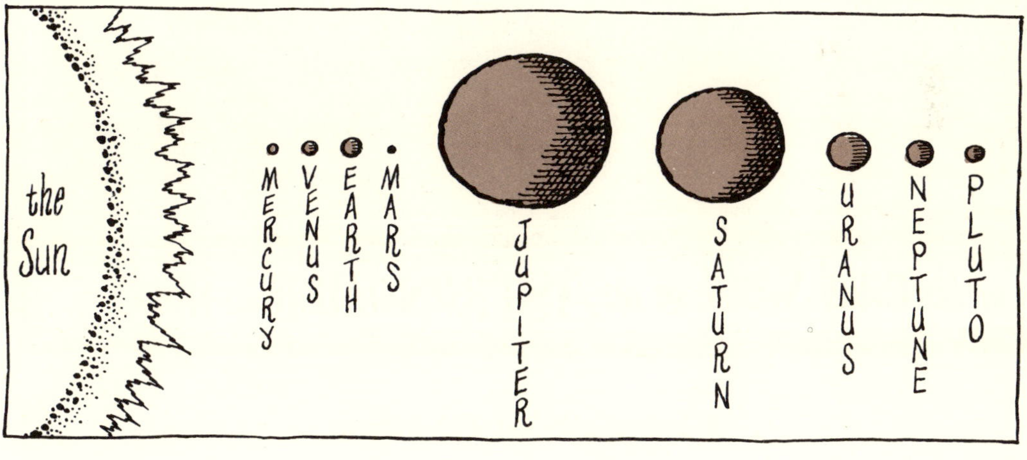

Ancient people believed stars and planets influenced human events. That belief is called ASTROLOGY. Some modern peoples believe they are ancient peoples because they still believe in Astrology. The date of a person's birth is important to Astrologers. Here is a chart of the signs of the ZODIAC:

ARIES the RAM starts March 21

TAURUS the BULL April 20

GEMINI the TWINS May 21

CANCER the CRAB June 22

LEO the LION July 23

VIRGO the VIRGIN August 23

LIBRA the BALANCE September 23

SCORPIO the SCORPION October 24

SAGITTARIUS the ARCHER November 22

CAPRICORN the GOAT December 22

AQUARIUS the WATER BEARER January 20

PISCES the FISHES February 19

Knowledge of the positions of stars and planets are an aid in navigation.

THINGS TO LOOK FOR IN THE NIGHT SKIES

The moon which affects our tides and reflects the Sun's light.

Comets and meteors (shooting stars) which leave brilliant trails as they zip through space.

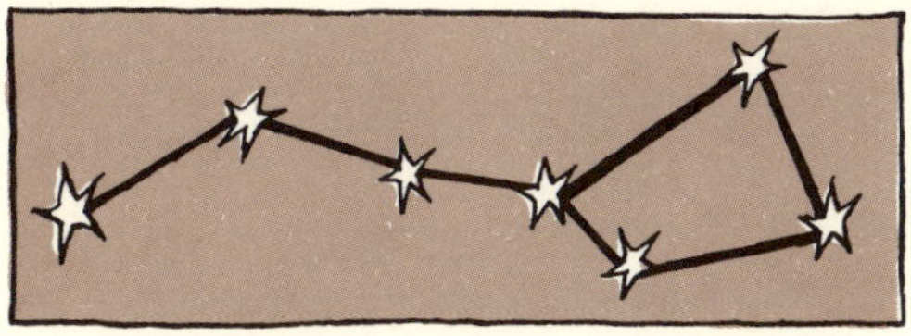

Constellations: familiar patterns of stars such as the "big dipper" (Ursa Major).

Bats, owls, nighthawks, lost balloons, and eight tiny reindeer so lively and quick.

With rocket exploration already at our command, there is no limit to what we might discover about outer space.

Scientists believe weather is formed by the effects of temperature, air pressure, wind, moisture, etc., on each other. Scientists will believe anything.

Other people believe weather is made by little old ladies who are mad at the whole world.

The truth is that weather is made by Santa's elves during their slack season.

The study of weather is called METEOROLOGY. Meteorologists study everything in the atmosphere which makes climate.

An amateur meteorologist taking a poll.

A meteorologist studying conditions.

An amateur meteorologist taking another poll.

Meteorologists give forecasts on television.

An amateur meteorologist-bore drowning in his own poll.

Meteorological equipment we use, know, and love:

Barometer Thermometer Weather Vane Breath

Open Window A Wet Finger Leaking Roof

SCIENTIFIC THINGS TO SAY ABOUT WEATHER

1. Equinox!
2. Precipitation!
3. Want your sidewalk shoveled for two dollars, lady?
4. Barometric pressure!
5. It's good for the farmers.
6. The picnic's called off.
7. Those farmers always were disgusting.
8. Rain, rain, go away, come again another day.
9. Not *this* another day—*another* another day.
10. What's it doing outside?
11. Well, then, do you want your sidewalk shoveled for a dollar, lady?
12. What's "precipitation"?

The study of ancient civilizations is the work of ARCHAEOLOGISTS. The study of archaeologists is the work of PSYCHOLOGISTS.

Archaeologists were unemployed until things got ancient enough for them to study.

Through the use of carbon-14 dating, archaeologists can tell how old an object is.

By finding and studying sites of former civilizations, archaeologists can give us a pretty good idea of what life was like in that place and period.

If ancient trees are near, a knowledgeable study of their growth rings will give clues to the climate at specific times. This study is called DENDROCHRONOLOGY by everyone who can pronounce all of it.

Through the ages, cities have tended to become covered over. New cities were built above where the old ones stood. Digging through the layers, archaeologists find the hidden past of a civilization.

An Archaeological QUIZ

A. The figure at left is:
1. Ancient Egyptian.
2. An Eskimo hugging herself.
3. A long way from Tipperary.
4. George Washington crossing the Delaware.

B. The building at right is:
1. City Hall
2. A broken escalator.
3. A Mayan pyramid temple.
4. Albert C. Drngblv.

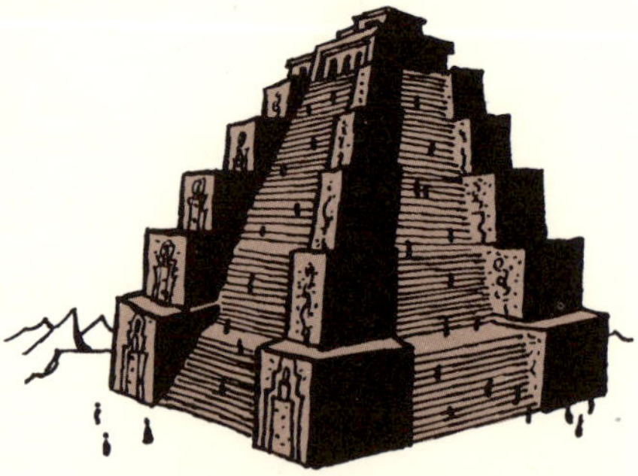

C. The Sphinx at left is:
1. An Eskimo *not* hugging herself.
2. George Washington Crossing the Delaware.
3. A Sphinx at left.
4. George Washington re-crossing the Delaware.

D. The ridiculous figure at the right is:
1. A babbling Sphinx.
2. The King's English.
3. George Washington crossing his eyes.
4. Galileo in the wrong part of this book.

ANSWERS: A:1; B:3; C:3; D:4. If you had none or more right, you have nothing to brag about.

The MIND

is an aspect of that amazing control center of the body: the BRAIN.

The human mind, which started the study of science, has always prompted scientific curiosity about itself.

One day a lady thought she saw a snake coming through the wall.

She went to see Dr. Sigmund Freud—and PSYCHIATRY was born.

One theory is that thought and behavior are guided by the SUBconscious mind—called the ID.

The EGO is the conscious idea of one's self. The LIBIDO is the subconscious urge to survive.

The study of the human mind has a long way to go. But then, again, so has the human mind. They both need all the help they can get.

But we've got to know what we're doing.

As long as there is more to know, man will want to know more. Man will always seek the truth. And SCIENCE will march forward, anyway.

SCIENCE MARCHING FORWARD, ANYWAY.

TIME
MATHEMATICS
CELLS
ELECTRICITY
The
Chemistry
MEDICINE
SOUND
SPACE
LENSES &
PRISMS
The